Finding Colors

Green

Moira Anderson

Heinemann Library
Chicago, Illinois

© 2006 Heinemann Library
a division of Reed Elsevier Inc.
Chicago, Illinois

Customer Service 888-454-2279
Visit our website at www.heinemannlibrary.com

Editorial: Moira Anderson, Carmel Heron
Page layout: Marta White, Heinemann Library Australia
Photo research: Jes Senbergs, Wendy Duncan
Production: Tracey Jarrett
Printed and bound in China by South China Printing Company Ltd.

09 08 07 06
10 9 8 7 6 5 4 3 2 1   8698

Library of Congress Cataloging-in-Publication Data
Anderson, Moira (Moira Wilshin)
 Green / Moira Anderson.
     p. cm. -- (Finding colors)
 Includes index.
 ISBN 1-4034-7445-1 (lib. bdg. : alk. paper) -- ISBN 1-4034-7450-8 (pbk. : alk. paper)
 1. Green--Juvenile literature. 2. Colors--Juvenile literature. I. Title.
II. Series: Anderson, Moira (Moira Wilshin). Finding colors.
  QC495.5.A534 2005
  535.6--dc22
                                                    2005009690

Acknowledgments
The author and publisher are grateful to the following for permission to reproduce copyright
material: Rob Cruse Photography: pp. **6, 8, 10, 11**; Corbis: pp. **22, 24**; Getty Images: p. **16**; Getty
Images/PhotoDisc: p. **15**, /National Geographic/George Grall: pp. **20, 23**; PhotoDisc, pp. **4, 5, 7,
9, 12, 13, 14, 18, 19, 20, 21, 23** (all except frog feet); photolibrary.com/Plainpicture: p. **17**.

Front cover photograph permission of Tudor Photography, back cover photographs permission
of Getty Images/National Geographic/George Grall (frog) and PhotoDisc (grapes).

Every effort has been made to contact copyright holders of any material reproduced in this book.
Any omissions will be rectified in subsequent printings if notice is given to the publisher.

Many thanks to the teachers, library media specialists, reading instructors, and educational
consultants who have helped develop the Read and Learn/Lee y aprende brand.

Contents

Some words are shown in bold, **like this**.
You can find them in the glossary on page 23.

What Is Green?

Green is a color.

What different colors can you see in this picture?

The color green is all around.

What green things can you see
in this picture?

What Green Things Can I Eat?

When green pears are soft,
we can eat them.

These grapes are green.

Grapes grow in bunches.

What Other Green Foods Can I Eat?

Green lettuce is good on a sandwich.

Lettuce is good in salads too.

These green beans are long
and crunchy.

Most people cook green beans
to eat them.

What Green Things Are There at Home?

This couch is green.

It is soft and comfy to sit on.

This glass is green.

Glass is hard and smooth.

What Is Green in the Garden?

blades

There is green grass in the garden.

The **blades** of grass are green.

These herbs are green.

Herbs are put in food to add **flavor**.

What Else Is Green in the Garden?

This hose is green.

It is used to water the **plants**.

This watering can is green.

It is used to water the plants too.

Water helps the plants to grow.

What Is Green at the Playground?

This merry-go-round is green.

It goes round and round.

This toy is green.

It goes backwards and forwards.

What Green Things Grow?

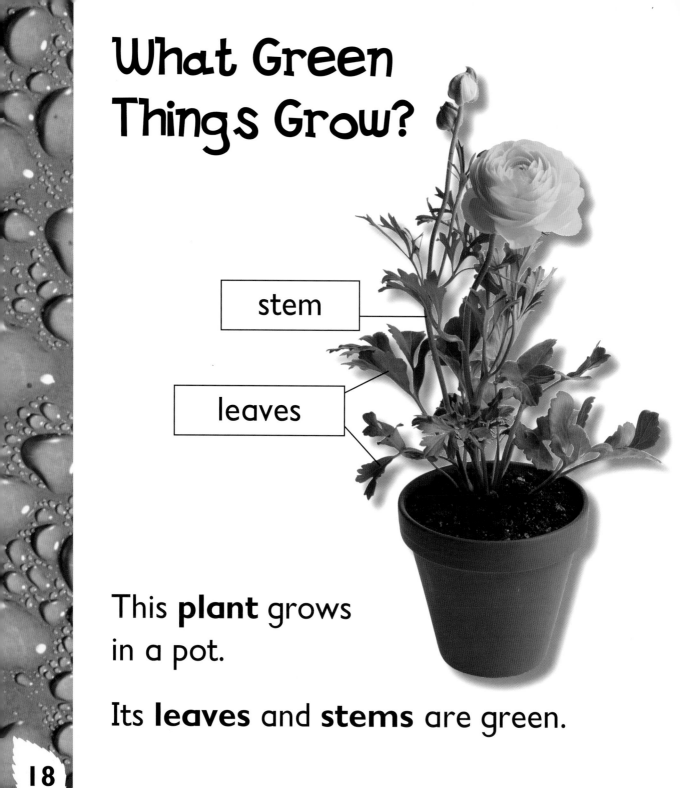

stem

leaves

This **plant** grows
in a pot.

Its **leaves** and **stems** are green.

These green plants grow in the pond.

The big flat leaves float on top of
the water.

Are There Green Animals?

This frog is green.

The **suckers** on its feet help it climb.

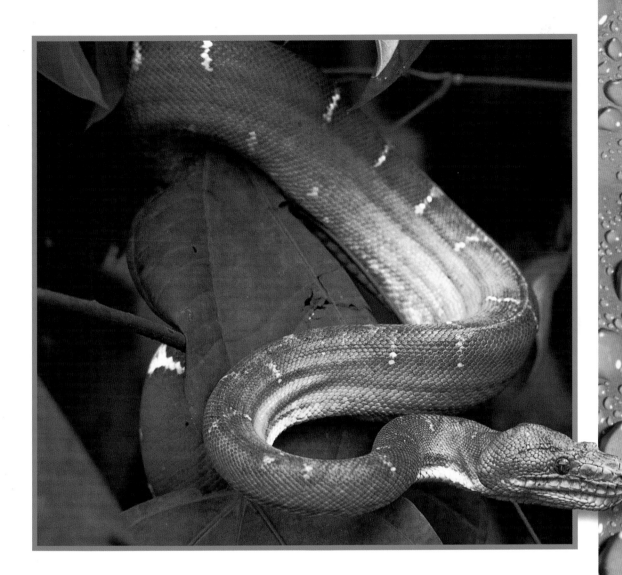

This snake is green.

It can be hard to see this snake on green plants.

Quiz

What green things can you see?

Look for the answers on page 24.

Glossary

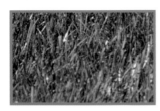

blade
flat, thin leaf

flavor
taste of something you eat

leaf
flat part of a plant that grows
from the stem

plant
living thing that cannot move; most
need soil, water, and sun to grow

stem
part of a plant where the
flowers and leaves grow

sucker
sticky pad that holds on to things

Index

Answers to the quiz on page 22

trees

T-shirt

grass

Notes to parents and teachers

Reading non-fiction texts for information is an important part of a child's literacy development. Readers can be encouraged to ask simple questions and then use the text to find the answers. Each chapter in this book begins with a question. Read the questions together. Look at the pictures. Talk about what the answer might be. Then read the text to find out if your predictions were correct. To develop readers' enquiry skills, encourage them to think of other questions they might ask about the topic. Discuss where you could find the answers. Assist children in using the contents page, picture glossary and index to practise research skills and new vocabulary.